BUCKET LIST

100 Things I Want To See or Do Before the Sun Sets on My Life!

Rosemary Augustine

BUCKET LIST

100 Things I Want To See or Do Before the Sun Sets on My Life!

Book Designer and Author: Rosemary Augustine

Copyright © Rosemary Augustine 2015

All Rights Reserved. No part of this book may be reproduced or transmitted in any form or by any means, electronic or mechanical, including photocopying, faxing, recording, emailing, posting on social media or by any information storage and retrieval system, or used for any other purpose without written permission from the author.

Published by:
Blue Spruce Publishing Company
2175 Golf Isle Drive, Suite 1024
Melbourne, FL 32935
610.647.8863
info@BlueSprucePublishing.com

Cover Design: Rosemary Augustine
Author Photo: Elsie Koenig
Graphics: Provided by OpenClipArt.org

ISBN 13: 978-1-943581-02-3

ISBN 10: 1-9435810-2-9

How to Use This Book

This book is designed so that you can list the things you want to see, do, or accomplish before the sun sets on your life (or before you die). The first 2 pages offers you a list of numbers - 1-100 - so you can list those things and keep track of the things you want to see, do or accomplish. The remaining pages offer you a 2 page journal (see the corresponding number in the box on the top of the page that matches the number on the 1-100 list). The first page provides space to write about your experience - what you did, where you did it and who was with you at the time, along with your thoughts and feelings. On the back side of the page are lines and a box. The lines give you space to continue to write about your experience. The box offers you a place to either draw a picture, paste a picture or paste / tape memorabilia from your experience. Let's say one of your bucket list items is to see a particular sports team play in a certain stadium… you can paste your ticket or other items from that day's sporting event in that box.

You don't have to list all 100 things at once. Add to the list when you decide that you want to add it to your bucket list. Then when you complete that item number, go to the corresponding number within the journal and write about your experience.

This **Bucket List** book is an opportunity to have a place to keep your memories of people to meet, places to see and things to do in your life that are important or have meaning for you to accomplish. Dreams, passion, desires… whatever you want to call it, this is the place to keep the record and watch your life unfold over the years as you complete all 100. Some people have completed the first 100 and have started an additional 100. Others are still working on their first 100. Wherever you are in the process, let this be a place to hold those memories. And a place you can return to time and again to remind yourself, "I did that!"

Bucket List #s 1-50

- ☐ 1. _____
- ☐ 2. _____
- ☐ 3. _____
- ☐ 4. _____
- ☐ 5. _____
- ☐ 6. _____
- ☐ 7. _____
- ☐ 8. _____
- ☐ 9. _____
- ☐ 10. _____
- ☐ 11. _____
- ☐ 12. _____
- ☐ 13. _____
- ☐ 14. _____
- ☐ 15. _____
- ☐ 16. _____
- ☐ 17. _____
- ☐ 18. _____
- ☐ 19. _____
- ☐ 20. _____
- ☐ 21. _____
- ☐ 22. _____
- ☐ 23. _____
- ☐ 24. _____
- ☐ 25. _____
- ☐ 26. _____
- ☐ 27. _____
- ☐ 28. _____
- ☐ 29. _____
- ☐ 30. _____
- ☐ 31. _____
- ☐ 32. _____
- ☐ 33. _____
- ☐ 34. _____
- ☐ 35. _____
- ☐ 36. _____
- ☐ 37. _____
- ☐ 38. _____
- ☐ 39. _____
- ☐ 40. _____
- ☐ 41. _____
- ☐ 42. _____
- ☐ 43. _____
- ☐ 44. _____
- ☐ 45. _____
- ☐ 46. _____
- ☐ 47. _____
- ☐ 48. _____
- ☐ 49. _____
- ☐ 50. _____

Bucket List - #s 51-100

- [ ] 51. _____
- [ ] 52. _____
- [ ] 53. _____
- [ ] 54. _____
- [ ] 55. _____
- [ ] 56. _____
- [ ] 57. _____
- [ ] 58. _____
- [ ] 59. _____
- [ ] 60. _____
- [ ] 61. _____
- [ ] 62. _____
- [ ] 63. _____
- [ ] 64. _____
- [ ] 65. _____
- [ ] 66. _____
- [ ] 67. _____
- [ ] 68. _____
- [ ] 69. _____
- [ ] 70. _____
- [ ] 71. _____
- [ ] 72. _____
- [ ] 73. _____
- [ ] 74. _____
- [ ] 75. _____
- [ ] 76. _____
- [ ] 77. _____
- [ ] 78. _____
- [ ] 79. _____
- [ ] 80. _____
- [ ] 81. _____
- [ ] 82. _____
- [ ] 83. _____
- [ ] 84. _____
- [ ] 85. _____
- [ ] 86. _____
- [ ] 87. _____
- [ ] 88. _____
- [ ] 89. _____
- [ ] 90. _____
- [ ] 91. _____
- [ ] 92. _____
- [ ] 93. _____
- [ ] 94. _____
- [ ] 95. _____
- [ ] 96. _____
- [ ] 97. _____
- [ ] 98. _____
- [ ] 99. _____
- [ ] 100. _____

#1

Date: _____

Description: _____
_____

Why I did this: _____
_____

Location (or where I completed): _____
_____

Who accompanied me: _____
_____

My thoughts: _____
_____
_____

My feelings: _____
_____
_____

Will I do it again:

☐ Yes … ☐ No … ☐ Maybe … ☐ Never … ☐ With someone … ☐ With someone else …

Why: _____
_____
_____

On the back of this page, you have a space for Journal notes including lines and even a place to draw about your experience.

Additional Space To Write, Draw and/or Add Additional Thoughts or Memorabilia About Your Experience.

#2

Date: _____

Description: _____
_____

Why I did this: _____
_____

Location (or where I completed): _____
_____

Who accompanied me: _____
_____

My thoughts: _____
_____
_____

My feelings: _____
_____
_____

Will I do it again:

☐ Yes … ☐ No … ☐ Maybe … ☐ Never … ☐ With someone … ☐ With someone else …

Why: _____
_____
_____

On the back of this page, you have a space for Journal notes including lines and even a place to draw about your experience. ➲

Additional Space To Write, Draw and/or Add Additional Thoughts or Memorabilia About Your Experience.

#3

Date: _____

Description: _____
_____

Why I did this: _____
_____

Location (or where I completed): _____
_____

Who accompanied me: _____
_____

My thoughts: _____
_____
_____
_____

My feelings: _____
_____
_____
_____

Will I do it again:

☐ Yes … ☐ No … ☐ Maybe … ☐ Never … ☐ With someone … ☐ With someone else …

Why: _____
_____
_____

On the back of this page, you have a space for Journal notes including lines and even a place to draw about your experience. ➲

Additional Space To Write, Draw and/or Add Additional Thoughts or Memorabilia About Your Experience.

#4

Date: _____

Description: _____
_____

Why I did this: _____
_____

Location (or where I completed): _____
_____

Who accompanied me: _____
_____

My thoughts: _____
_____
_____

My feelings: _____
_____
_____

Will I do it again:

☐ Yes … ☐ No … ☐ Maybe … ☐ Never … ☐ With someone … ☐ With someone else …

Why: _____
_____
_____

On the back of this page, you have a space for Journal notes including lines and even a place to draw about your experience. ➲

Additional Space To Write, Draw and/or Add Additional Thoughts or Memorabilia About Your Experience.

#5

Date: _____

Description: _____
_____

Why I did this: _____
_____

Location (or where I completed): _____
_____

Who accompanied me: _____
_____

My thoughts: _____
_____
_____

My feelings: _____
_____
_____

Will I do it again:

☐ Yes … ☐ No … ☐ Maybe … ☐ Never … ☐ With someone … ☐ With someone else …

Why: _____
_____
_____

On the back of this page, you have a space for Journal notes including lines and even a place to draw about your experience. ↻

Additional Space To Write, Draw and/or Add Additional Thoughts or Memorabilia About Your Experience.

#6

Date: _____

Description: _____
_____

Why I did this: _____
_____

Location (or where I completed): _____
_____

Who accompanied me: _____
_____

My thoughts: _____
_____
_____

My feelings: _____
_____
_____

Will I do it again:

☐ Yes … ☐ No … ☐ Maybe … ☐ Never … ☐ With someone … ☐ With someone else …

Why: _____
_____
_____

On the back of this page, you have a space for Journal notes including lines and even a place to draw about your experience.

Additional Space To Write, Draw and/or Add Additional Thoughts or Memorabilia About Your Experience.

#7

Date: _____

Description: _____
_____

Why I did this: _____
_____

Location (or where I completed): _____
_____

Who accompanied me: _____
_____

My thoughts: _____
_____
_____
_____

My feelings: _____
_____
_____
_____

Will I do it again:

☐ Yes … ☐ No … ☐ Maybe … ☐ Never … ☐ With someone … ☐ With someone else …

Why: _____
_____
_____

On the back of this page, you have a space for Journal notes including lines and even a place to draw about your experience. ➲

Additional Space To Write, Draw and/or Add Additional Thoughts or Memorabilia About Your Experience.

#8

Date: _____

Description: _____
_____

Why I did this: _____
_____

Location (or where I completed): _____
_____

Who accompanied me: _____
_____

My thoughts: _____
_____
_____

My feelings: _____
_____
_____

Will I do it again:

☐ Yes … ☐ No … ☐ Maybe … ☐ Never … ☐ With someone … ☐ With someone else …

Why: _____
_____
_____

On the back of this page, you have a space for Journal notes including lines and even a place to draw about your experience. ↻

Additional Space To Write, Draw and/or Add Additional Thoughts or Memorabilia About Your Experience.

#9

Date: _____

Description: _____
_____

Why I did this: _____
_____

Location (or where I completed): _____
_____

Who accompanied me: _____
_____

My thoughts: _____
_____
_____

My feelings: _____
_____
_____

Will I do it again:

☐ Yes … ☐ No … ☐ Maybe … ☐ Never … ☐ With someone … ☐ With someone else …

Why: _____
_____
_____

On the back of this page, you have a space for Journal notes including lines and even a place to draw about your experience.

Additional Space To Write, Draw and/or Add Additional Thoughts or Memorabilia About Your Experience.

10

Date: _____

Description: _____
_____

Why I did this: _____
_____

Location (or where I completed): _____
_____

Who accompanied me: _____
_____

My thoughts: _____
_____
_____

My feelings: _____
_____
_____

Will I do it again:

☐ Yes … ☐ No … ☐ Maybe … ☐ Never … ☐ With someone … ☐ With someone else …

Why: _____
_____
_____

On the back of this page, you have a space for Journal notes including lines and even a place to draw about your experience. ➲

Additional Space To Write, Draw and/or Add Additional Thoughts or Memorabilia About Your Experience.

#11

Date: _____

Description: _____
_____

Why I did this: _____
_____

Location (or where I completed): _____
_____

Who accompanied me: _____
_____

My thoughts: _____
_____
_____

My feelings: _____
_____
_____

Will I do it again:

☐ Yes … ☐ No … ☐ Maybe … ☐ Never … ☐ With someone … ☐ With someone else …

Why: _____
_____
_____

On the back of this page, you have a space for Journal notes including lines and even a place to draw about your experience. ➲

Additional Space To Write, Draw and/or Add Additional Thoughts or Memorabilia About Your Experience.

12

Date: _____

Description: _____
_____

Why I did this: _____
_____

Location (or where I completed): _____
_____

Who accompanied me: _____
_____

My thoughts: _____
_____
_____
_____

My feelings: _____
_____
_____
_____

Will I do it again:

☐ Yes … ☐ No … ☐ Maybe … ☐ Never … ☐ With someone … ☐ With someone else …

Why: _____
_____
_____

On the back of this page, you have a space for Journal notes including lines and even a place to draw about your experience.

Additional Space To Write, Draw and/or Add Additional Thoughts or Memorabilia About Your Experience.

#13

Date: _____

Description: _____
_____

Why I did this: _____
_____

Location (or where I completed): _____
_____

Who accompanied me: _____
_____

My thoughts: _____
_____
_____
_____

My feelings: _____
_____
_____
_____

Will I do it again:

☐ Yes … ☐ No … ☐ Maybe … ☐ Never … ☐ With someone … ☐ With someone else …

Why: _____
_____
_____

On the back of this page, you have a space for Journal notes including lines and even a place to draw about your experience. ➲

Additional Space To Write, Draw and/or Add Additional Thoughts or Memorabilia About Your Experience.

14

Date: _____

Description: _____
_____

Why I did this: _____
_____

Location (or where I completed): _____
_____

Who accompanied me: _____
_____

My thoughts: _____
_____
_____
_____

My feelings: _____
_____
_____
_____

Will I do it again:

☐ Yes … ☐ No … ☐ Maybe … ☐ Never … ☐ With someone … ☐ With someone else …

Why: _____
_____
_____

On the back of this page, you have a space for Journal notes including lines and even a place to draw about your experience.

Additional Space To Write, Draw and/or Add Additional Thoughts or Memorabilia About Your Experience.

15

Date: _____

Description: _____
_____

Why I did this: _____
_____

Location (or where I completed): _____
_____

Who accompanied me: _____
_____

My thoughts: _____
_____
_____

My feelings: _____
_____
_____

Will I do it again:

☐ Yes ... ☐ No ... ☐ Maybe ... ☐ Never ... ☐ With someone ... ☐ With someone else ...

Why: _____
_____
_____

On the back of this page, you have a space for Journal notes including lines and even a place to draw about your experience. ➲

Additional Space To Write, Draw and/or Add Additional Thoughts or Memorabilia About Your Experience.

16

Date: _____

Description: _____
_____

Why I did this: _____
_____

Location (or where I completed): _____
_____

Who accompanied me: _____
_____

My thoughts: _____
_____
_____
_____

My feelings: _____
_____
_____
_____

Will I do it again:

☐ Yes … ☐ No … ☐ Maybe … ☐ Never … ☐ With someone … ☐ With someone else …

Why: _____
_____
_____

On the back of this page, you have a space for Journal notes including lines and even a place to draw about your experience.

Additional Space To Write, Draw and/or Add Additional Thoughts or Memorabilia About Your Experience.

#17

Date: _____

Description: _____
_____

Why I did this: _____
_____

Location (or where I completed): _____
_____

Who accompanied me: _____
_____

My thoughts: _____
_____
_____

My feelings: _____
_____
_____

Will I do it again:

☐ Yes … ☐ No … ☐ Maybe … ☐ Never … ☐ With someone … ☐ With someone else …

Why: _____
_____
_____

On the back of this page, you have a space for Journal notes including lines and even a place to draw about your experience.

Additional Space To Write, Draw and/or Add Additional Thoughts or Memorabilia About Your Experience.

#18

Date: _____

Description: _____
_____

Why I did this: _____
_____

Location (or where I completed): _____
_____

Who accompanied me: _____
_____

My thoughts: _____
_____
_____

My feelings: _____
_____
_____

Will I do it again:

☐ Yes … ☐ No … ☐ Maybe … ☐ Never … ☐ With someone … ☐ With someone else …

Why: _____
_____
_____

On the back of this page, you have a space for Journal notes including lines and even a place to draw about your experience.

Additional Space To Write, Draw and/or Add Additional Thoughts or Memorabilia About Your Experience.

19

Date: _____

Description: _____
_____

Why I did this: _____
_____

Location (or where I completed): _____
_____

Who accompanied me: _____
_____

My thoughts: _____
_____
_____

My feelings: _____
_____
_____

Will I do it again:

☐ Yes … ☐ No … ☐ Maybe … ☐ Never … ☐ With someone … ☐ With someone else …

Why: _____
_____
_____

On the back of this page, you have a space for Journal notes including lines and even a place to draw about your experience. ↻

Additional Space To Write, Draw and/or Add Additional Thoughts or Memorabilia About Your Experience.

20

Date: _____

Description: _____
_____

Why I did this: _____
_____

Location (or where I completed): _____
_____

Who accompanied me: _____
_____

My thoughts: _____
_____
_____

My feelings: _____
_____
_____

Will I do it again:

☐ Yes … ☐ No … ☐ Maybe … ☐ Never … ☐ With someone … ☐ With someone else …

Why: _____
_____
_____

On the back of this page, you have a space for Journal notes including lines and even a place to draw about your experience.

Additional Space To Write, Draw and/or Add Additional Thoughts or Memorabilia About Your Experience.

21

Date: _____

Description: _____
_____

Why I did this: _____
_____

Location (or where I completed): _____
_____

Who accompanied me: _____
_____

My thoughts: _____
_____
_____

My feelings: _____
_____
_____

Will I do it again:

☐ Yes … ☐ No … ☐ Maybe … ☐ Never … ☐ With someone … ☐ With someone else …

Why: _____
_____
_____

On the back of this page, you have a space for Journal notes including lines and even a place to draw about your experience.

Additional Space To Write, Draw and/or Add Additional Thoughts or Memorabilia About Your Experience.

22

Date: _____

Description: _____
_____

Why I did this: _____
_____

Location (or where I completed): _____
_____

Who accompanied me: _____
_____

My thoughts: _____
_____
_____

My feelings: _____
_____
_____

Will I do it again:

☐ Yes … ☐ No … ☐ Maybe … ☐ Never … ☐ With someone … ☐ With someone else …

Why: _____
_____
_____

On the back of this page, you have a space for Journal notes including lines and even a place to draw about your experience.

Additional Space To Write, Draw and/or Add Additional Thoughts or Memorabilia About Your Experience.

#23

Date: _____

Description: _____
_____

Why I did this: _____
_____

Location (or where I completed): _____
_____

Who accompanied me: _____
_____

My thoughts: _____
_____
_____

My feelings: _____
_____
_____

Will I do it again:

☐ Yes … ☐ No … ☐ Maybe … ☐ Never … ☐ With someone … ☐ With someone else …

Why: _____
_____
_____

On the back of this page, you have a space for Journal notes including lines and even a place to draw about your experience. ➲

Additional Space To Write, Draw and/or Add Additional Thoughts or Memorabilia About Your Experience.

#24

Date: _____

Description: _____
_____

Why I did this: _____
_____

Location (or where I completed): _____
_____

Who accompanied me: _____
_____

My thoughts: _____
_____
_____
_____

My feelings: _____
_____
_____
_____

Will I do it again:

☐ Yes … ☐ No … ☐ Maybe … ☐ Never … ☐ With someone … ☐ With someone else …

Why: _____
_____
_____

On the back of this page, you have a space for Journal notes including lines and even a place to draw about your experience.

Additional Space To Write, Draw and/or Add Additional Thoughts or Memorabilia About Your Experience.

25

Date: _____

Description: _____
_____

Why I did this: _____
_____

Location (or where I completed): _____
_____

Who accompanied me: _____
_____

My thoughts: _____
_____
_____

My feelings: _____
_____
_____

Will I do it again:

☐ Yes … ☐ No … ☐ Maybe … ☐ Never … ☐ With someone … ☐ With someone else …

Why: _____
_____
_____

On the back of this page, you have a space for Journal notes including lines and even a place to draw about your experience.   ➲

Additional Space To Write, Draw and/or Add Additional Thoughts or Memorabilia About Your Experience.

26

Date: _____

Description: _____
_____

Why I did this: _____
_____

Location (or where I completed): _____
_____

Who accompanied me: _____
_____

My thoughts: _____
_____
_____

My feelings: _____
_____
_____

Will I do it again:

☐ Yes … ☐ No … ☐ Maybe … ☐ Never … ☐ With someone … ☐ With someone else …

Why: _____
_____
_____

On the back of this page, you have a space for Journal notes including lines and even a place to draw about your experience. ➲

Additional Space To Write, Draw and/or Add Additional Thoughts or Memorabilia About Your Experience.

27

Date: _____

Description: _____
_____

Why I did this: _____
_____

Location (or where I completed): _____
_____

Who accompanied me: _____
_____

My thoughts: _____
_____
_____

My feelings: _____
_____
_____

Will I do it again:

☐ Yes … ☐ No … ☐ Maybe … ☐ Never … ☐ With someone … ☐ With someone else …

Why: _____
_____
_____

On the back of this page, you have a space for Journal notes including lines and even a place to draw about your experience. ⤴

Additional Space To Write, Draw and/or Add Additional Thoughts or Memorabilia About Your Experience.

28

Date: _____

Description: _____
_____

Why I did this: _____
_____

Location (or where I completed): _____
_____

Who accompanied me: _____
_____

My thoughts: _____
_____
_____
_____

My feelings: _____
_____
_____
_____

Will I do it again:

☐ Yes … ☐ No … ☐ Maybe … ☐ Never … ☐ With someone … ☐ With someone else …

Why: _____
_____
_____

On the back of this page, you have a space for Journal notes including lines and even a place to draw about your experience. ⮕

Additional Space To Write, Draw and/or Add Additional Thoughts or Memorabilia About Your Experience.

29

Date: _____

Description: _____
_____

Why I did this: _____
_____

Location (or where I completed): _____
_____

Who accompanied me: _____
_____

My thoughts: _____
_____
_____

My feelings: _____
_____
_____

Will I do it again:

☐ Yes … ☐ No … ☐ Maybe … ☐ Never … ☐ With someone … ☐ With someone else …

Why: _____
_____
_____

On the back of this page, you have a space for Journal notes including lines and even a place to draw about your experience. ↻

Additional Space To Write, Draw and/or Add Additional Thoughts or Memorabilia About Your Experience.

30

Date: _____

Description: _____
_____

Why I did this: _____
_____

Location (or where I completed): _____
_____

Who accompanied me: _____
_____

My thoughts: _____
_____
_____

My feelings: _____
_____
_____

Will I do it again:

☐ Yes … ☐ No … ☐ Maybe … ☐ Never … ☐ With someone … ☐ With someone else …

Why: _____
_____
_____

On the back of this page, you have a space for Journal notes including lines and even a place to draw about your experience. ➲

Additional Space To Write, Draw and/or Add Additional Thoughts or Memorabilia About Your Experience.

#31

Date: _____

Description: _____
_____

Why I did this: _____
_____

Location (or where I completed): _____
_____

Who accompanied me: _____
_____

My thoughts: _____
_____
_____

My feelings: _____
_____
_____

Will I do it again:

☐ Yes … ☐ No … ☐ Maybe … ☐ Never … ☐ With someone … ☐ With someone else …

Why: _____
_____
_____

On the back of this page, you have a space for Journal notes including lines and even a place to draw about your experience. ⮕

Additional Space To Write, Draw and/or Add Additional Thoughts or Memorabilia About Your Experience.

32

Date: _____

Description: _____
_____

Why I did this: _____
_____

Location (or where I completed): _____
_____

Who accompanied me: _____
_____

My thoughts: _____
_____
_____

My feelings: _____
_____
_____

Will I do it again:

☐ Yes … ☐ No … ☐ Maybe … ☐ Never … ☐ With someone … ☐ With someone else …

Why: _____
_____
_____

On the back of this page, you have a space for Journal notes including lines and even a place to draw about your experience. ➲

Additional Space To Write, Draw and/or Add Additional Thoughts or Memorabilia About Your Experience.

33

Date: _____

Description: _____
_____

Why I did this: _____
_____

Location (or where I completed): _____
_____

Who accompanied me: _____
_____

My thoughts: _____
_____
_____
_____

My feelings: _____
_____
_____

Will I do it again:

☐ Yes ... ☐ No ... ☐ Maybe ... ☐ Never ... ☐ With someone ... ☐ With someone else ...

Why: _____
_____
_____

On the back of this page, you have a space for Journal notes including lines and even a place to draw about your experience. ⮕

Additional Space To Write, Draw and/or Add Additional Thoughts or Memorabilia About Your Experience.

34

Date: _____

Description: _____
_____

Why I did this: _____
_____

Location (or where I completed): _____
_____

Who accompanied me: _____
_____

My thoughts: _____
_____
_____
_____

My feelings: _____
_____
_____
_____

Will I do it again:

☐ Yes … ☐ No … ☐ Maybe … ☐ Never … ☐ With someone … ☐ With someone else …

Why: _____
_____
_____

On the back of this page, you have a space for Journal notes including lines and even a place to draw about your experience. ➲

Additional Space To Write, Draw and/or Add Additional Thoughts or Memorabilia About Your Experience.

35

Date: _____

Description: _____
_____

Why I did this: _____
_____

Location (or where I completed): _____
_____

Who accompanied me: _____
_____

My thoughts: _____
_____
_____

My feelings: _____
_____
_____

Will I do it again:

☐ Yes ... ☐ No ... ☐ Maybe ... ☐ Never ... ☐ With someone ... ☐ With someone else ...

Why: _____
_____
_____

On the back of this page, you have a space for Journal notes including lines and even a place to draw about your experience.   ↻

Additional Space To Write, Draw and/or Add Additional Thoughts or Memorabilia About Your Experience.

36

Date: _____

Description: _____
_____

Why I did this: _____
_____

Location (or where I completed): _____
_____

Who accompanied me: _____
_____

My thoughts: _____
_____
_____

My feelings: _____
_____
_____

Will I do it again:

☐ Yes … ☐ No … ☐ Maybe … ☐ Never … ☐ With someone … ☐ With someone else …

Why: _____
_____
_____

On the back of this page, you have a space for Journal notes including lines and even a place to draw about your experience. ⮑

Additional Space To Write, Draw and/or Add Additional Thoughts or Memorabilia About Your Experience.

37

Date: _____

Description: _____
_____

Why I did this: _____
_____

Location (or where I completed): _____
_____

Who accompanied me: _____
_____

My thoughts: _____
_____
_____
_____

My feelings: _____
_____
_____
_____

Will I do it again:

☐ Yes … ☐ No … ☐ Maybe … ☐ Never … ☐ With someone … ☐ With someone else …

Why: _____
_____
_____

On the back of this page, you have a space for Journal notes including lines and even a place to draw about your experience. ⟳

Additional Space To Write, Draw and/or Add Additional Thoughts or Memorabilia About Your Experience.

38

Date: _____

Description: _____
_____

Why I did this: _____
_____

Location (or where I completed): _____
_____

Who accompanied me: _____
_____

My thoughts: _____
_____
_____

My feelings: _____
_____
_____

Will I do it again:

☐ Yes ... ☐ No ... ☐ Maybe ... ☐ Never ... ☐ With someone ... ☐ With someone else ...

Why: _____
_____
_____

On the back of this page, you have a space for Journal notes including lines and even a place to draw about your experience.

Additional Space To Write, Draw and/or Add Additional Thoughts or Memorabilia About Your Experience.

#39

Date: _____

Description: _____
_____

Why I did this: _____
_____

Location (or where I completed): _____
_____

Who accompanied me: _____
_____

My thoughts: _____
_____
_____

My feelings: _____
_____
_____

Will I do it again:

☐ Yes … ☐ No … ☐ Maybe … ☐ Never … ☐ With someone … ☐ With someone else …

Why: _____
_____
_____

On the back of this page, you have a space for Journal notes including lines and even a place to draw about your experience. ➲

Additional Space To Write, Draw and/or Add Additional Thoughts or Memorabilia About Your Experience.

#40

Date: _____

Description: _____
_____

Why I did this: _____
_____

Location (or where I completed): _____
_____

Who accompanied me: _____
_____

My thoughts: _____
_____
_____

My feelings: _____
_____
_____

Will I do it again:

☐ Yes … ☐ No … ☐ Maybe … ☐ Never … ☐ With someone … ☐ With someone else …

Why: _____
_____
_____

On the back of this page, you have a space for Journal notes including lines and even a place to draw about your experience.

Additional Space To Write, Draw and/or Add Additional Thoughts or Memorabilia About Your Experience.

#41

Date: _____

Description: _____
_____

Why I did this: _____
_____

Location (or where I completed): _____
_____

Who accompanied me: _____
_____

My thoughts: _____
_____
_____

My feelings: _____
_____
_____

Will I do it again:

☐ Yes ... ☐ No ... ☐ Maybe ... ☐ Never ... ☐ With someone ... ☐ With someone else ...

Why: _____
_____
_____

On the back of this page, you have a space for Journal notes including lines and even a place to draw about your experience.

Additional Space To Write, Draw and/or Add Additional Thoughts or Memorabilia About Your Experience.

42

Date: _____

Description: _____
_____

Why I did this: _____
_____

Location (or where I completed): _____
_____

Who accompanied me: _____
_____

My thoughts: _____
_____
_____

My feelings: _____
_____
_____

Will I do it again:

☐ Yes … ☐ No … ☐ Maybe … ☐ Never … ☐ With someone … ☐ With someone else …

Why: _____
_____
_____

On the back of this page, you have a space for Journal notes including lines and even a place to draw about your experience.

Additional Space To Write, Draw and/or Add Additional Thoughts or Memorabilia About Your Experience.

43

Date: _____

Description: _____
_____

Why I did this: _____
_____

Location (or where I completed): _____
_____

Who accompanied me: _____
_____

My thoughts: _____
_____
_____
_____

My feelings: _____
_____
_____
_____

Will I do it again:

☐ Yes … ☐ No … ☐ Maybe … ☐ Never … ☐ With someone … ☐ With someone else …

Why: _____
_____
_____

On the back of this page, you have a space for Journal notes including lines and even a place to draw about your experience. ➲

Additional Space To Write, Draw and/or Add Additional Thoughts or Memorabilia About Your Experience.

44

Date: _____

Description: _____
_____

Why I did this: _____
_____

Location (or where I completed): _____
_____

Who accompanied me: _____
_____

My thoughts: _____
_____
_____

My feelings: _____
_____
_____

Will I do it again:

☐ Yes … ☐ No … ☐ Maybe … ☐ Never … ☐ With someone … ☐ With someone else …

Why: _____
_____
_____

On the back of this page, you have a space for Journal notes including lines and even a place to draw about your experience. ⮑

Additional Space To Write, Draw and/or Add Additional Thoughts or Memorabilia About Your Experience.

45

Date: _____

Description: _____
_____

Why I did this: _____
_____

Location (or where I completed): _____
_____

Who accompanied me: _____
_____

My thoughts: _____
_____
_____

My feelings: _____
_____
_____

Will I do it again:

☐ Yes … ☐ No … ☐ Maybe … ☐ Never … ☐ With someone … ☐ With someone else …

Why: _____
_____
_____

On the back of this page, you have a space for Journal notes including lines and even a place to draw about your experience. ➲

Additional Space To Write, Draw and/or Add Additional Thoughts or Memorabilia About Your Experience.

46

Date: _____

Description: _____
_____

Why I did this: _____
_____

Location (or where I completed): _____
_____

Who accompanied me: _____
_____

My thoughts: _____
_____
_____
_____

My feelings: _____
_____
_____
_____

Will I do it again:

☐ Yes … ☐ No … ☐ Maybe … ☐ Never … ☐ With someone … ☐ With someone else …

Why: _____
_____
_____

On the back of this page, you have a space for Journal notes including lines and even a place to draw about your experience. ➲

Additional Space To Write, Draw and/or Add Additional Thoughts or Memorabilia About Your Experience.

47

Date: _____

Description: _____
_____

Why I did this: _____
_____

Location (or where I completed): _____
_____

Who accompanied me: _____
_____

My thoughts: _____
_____
_____

My feelings: _____
_____
_____

Will I do it again:

☐ Yes ... ☐ No ... ☐ Maybe ... ☐ Never ... ☐ With someone ... ☐ With someone else ...

Why: _____
_____
_____

On the back of this page, you have a space for Journal notes including lines and even a place to draw about your experience. ⮑

Additional Space To Write, Draw and/or Add Additional Thoughts or Memorabilia About Your Experience.

48

Date: _____

Description: _____
_____

Why I did this: _____
_____

Location (or where I completed): _____
_____

Who accompanied me: _____
_____

My thoughts: _____
_____
_____

My feelings: _____
_____
_____

Will I do it again:

☐ Yes … ☐ No … ☐ Maybe … ☐ Never … ☐ With someone … ☐ With someone else …

Why: _____
_____
_____

On the back of this page, you have a space for Journal notes including lines and even a place to draw about your experience. ➲

Additional Space To Write, Draw and/or Add Additional Thoughts or Memorabilia About Your Experience.

49

Date: _____

Description: _____
_____

Why I did this: _____
_____

Location (or where I completed): _____
_____

Who accompanied me: _____
_____

My thoughts: _____
_____
_____

My feelings: _____
_____
_____

Will I do it again:

☐ Yes ... ☐ No ... ☐ Maybe ... ☐ Never ... ☐ With someone ... ☐ With someone else ...

Why: _____
_____
_____

On the back of this page, you have a space for Journal notes including lines and even a place to draw about your experience.

Additional Space To Write, Draw and/or Add Additional Thoughts or Memorabilia About Your Experience.

50

Date: _____

Description: _____
_____

Why I did this: _____
_____

Location (or where I completed): _____
_____

Who accompanied me: _____
_____

My thoughts: _____
_____
_____

My feelings: _____
_____
_____

Will I do it again:

☐ Yes … ☐ No … ☐ Maybe … ☐ Never … ☐ With someone … ☐ With someone else …

Why: _____
_____
_____

On the back of this page, you have a space for Journal notes including lines and even a place to draw about your experience. ↻

Additional Space To Write, Draw and/or Add Additional Thoughts or Memorabilia About Your Experience.

51

Date: _____

Description: _____
_____

Why I did this: _____
_____

Location (or where I completed): _____
_____

Who accompanied me: _____
_____

My thoughts: _____
_____
_____

My feelings: _____
_____
_____

Will I do it again:

☐ Yes … ☐ No … ☐ Maybe … ☐ Never … ☐ With someone … ☐ With someone else …

Why: _____
_____
_____

On the back of this page, you have a space for Journal notes including lines and even a place to draw about your experience.

Additional Space To Write, Draw and/or Add Additional Thoughts or Memorabilia About Your Experience.

52

Date: _____

Description: _____
_____

Why I did this: _____
_____

Location (or where I completed): _____
_____

Who accompanied me: _____
_____

My thoughts: _____
_____
_____
_____

My feelings: _____
_____
_____
_____

Will I do it again:

☐ Yes … ☐ No … ☐ Maybe … ☐ Never … ☐ With someone … ☐ With someone else …

Why: _____
_____
_____

On the back of this page, you have a space for Journal notes including lines and even a place to draw about your experience. ↻

Additional Space To Write, Draw and/or Add Additional Thoughts or Memorabilia About Your Experience.

53

Date: _____

Description: _____
_____

Why I did this: _____
_____

Location (or where I completed): _____
_____

Who accompanied me: _____
_____

My thoughts: _____
_____
_____

My feelings: _____
_____
_____

Will I do it again:

☐ Yes … ☐ No … ☐ Maybe … ☐ Never … ☐ With someone … ☐ With someone else …

Why: _____
_____
_____

On the back of this page, you have a space for Journal notes including lines and even a place to draw about your experience.

Additional Space To Write, Draw and/or Add Additional Thoughts or Memorabilia About Your Experience.

54

Date: _____

Description: _____
_____

Why I did this: _____
_____

Location (or where I completed): _____
_____

Who accompanied me: _____
_____

My thoughts: _____
_____
_____
_____

My feelings: _____
_____
_____
_____

Will I do it again:

☐ Yes … ☐ No … ☐ Maybe … ☐ Never … ☐ With someone … ☐ With someone else …

Why: _____
_____
_____

On the back of this page, you have a space for Journal notes including lines and even a place to draw about your experience. ➲

Additional Space To Write, Draw and/or Add Additional Thoughts or Memorabilia About Your Experience.

55

Date: _____

Description: _____

_____

Why I did this: _____

_____

Location (or where I completed): _____

_____

Who accompanied me: _____

_____

My thoughts: _____

_____

_____

My feelings: _____

_____

_____

Will I do it again:

☐ Yes … ☐ No … ☐ Maybe … ☐ Never … ☐ With someone … ☐ With someone else …

Why: _____

_____

_____

On the back of this page, you have a space for Journal notes including lines and even a place to draw about your experience. ↻

Additional Space To Write, Draw and/or Add Additional Thoughts or Memorabilia About Your Experience.

56

Date: _____

Description: _____
_____

Why I did this: _____
_____

Location (or where I completed): _____
_____

Who accompanied me: _____
_____

My thoughts: _____
_____
_____
_____

My feelings: _____
_____
_____
_____

Will I do it again:

☐ Yes … ☐ No … ☐ Maybe … ☐ Never … ☐ With someone … ☐ With someone else …

Why: _____
_____
_____

On the back of this page, you have a space for Journal notes including lines and even a place to draw about your experience. ➲

Additional Space To Write, Draw and/or Add Additional Thoughts or Memorabilia About Your Experience.

#57

Date: _____

Description: _____
_____

Why I did this: _____
_____

Location (or where I completed): _____
_____

Who accompanied me: _____
_____

My thoughts: _____
_____
_____

My feelings: _____
_____
_____

Will I do it again:

☐ Yes … ☐ No … ☐ Maybe … ☐ Never … ☐ With someone … ☐ With someone else …

Why: _____
_____
_____

On the back of this page, you have a space for Journal notes including lines and even a place to draw about your experience. ➲

Additional Space To Write, Draw and/or Add Additional Thoughts or Memorabilia About Your Experience.

58

Date: _____

Description: _____
_____

Why I did this: _____
_____

Location (or where I completed): _____
_____

Who accompanied me: _____
_____

My thoughts: _____
_____
_____

My feelings: _____
_____
_____

Will I do it again:

☐ Yes … ☐ No … ☐ Maybe … ☐ Never … ☐ With someone … ☐ With someone else …

Why: _____
_____
_____

On the back of this page, you have a space for Journal notes including lines and even a place to draw about your experience.

Additional Space To Write, Draw and/or Add Additional Thoughts or Memorabilia About Your Experience.

59

Date: _____

Description: _____
_____

Why I did this: _____
_____

Location (or where I completed): _____
_____

Who accompanied me: _____
_____

My thoughts: _____
_____
_____

My feelings: _____
_____
_____

Will I do it again:

☐ Yes … ☐ No … ☐ Maybe … ☐ Never … ☐ With someone … ☐ With someone else …

Why: _____
_____
_____

On the back of this page, you have a space for Journal notes including lines and even a place to draw about your experience. ➲

Additional Space To Write, Draw and/or Add Additional Thoughts or Memorabilia About Your Experience.

| # 60 |

Date: _____

Description: _____
_____

Why I did this: _____
_____

Location (or where I completed): _____
_____

Who accompanied me: _____
_____

My thoughts: _____
_____
_____

My feelings: _____
_____
_____

Will I do it again:

☐ Yes … ☐ No … ☐ Maybe … ☐ Never … ☐ With someone … ☐ With someone else …

Why: _____
_____
_____

On the back of this page, you have a space for Journal notes including lines and even a place to draw about your experience. ↻

Additional Space To Write, Draw and/or Add Additional Thoughts or Memorabilia About Your Experience.

#61

Date: _____

Description: _____
_____

Why I did this: _____
_____

Location (or where I completed): _____
_____

Who accompanied me: _____
_____

My thoughts: _____
_____
_____
_____

My feelings: _____
_____
_____

Will I do it again:

☐ Yes … ☐ No … ☐ Maybe … ☐ Never … ☐ With someone … ☐ With someone else …

Why: _____
_____
_____

On the back of this page, you have a space for Journal notes including lines and even a place to draw about your experience. ⮑

Additional Space To Write, Draw and/or Add Additional Thoughts or Memorabilia About Your Experience.

62

Date: _____

Description: _____
_____

Why I did this: _____
_____

Location (or where I completed): _____
_____

Who accompanied me: _____
_____

My thoughts: _____
_____
_____
_____

My feelings: _____
_____
_____
_____

Will I do it again:

☐ Yes … ☐ No … ☐ Maybe … ☐ Never … ☐ With someone … ☐ With someone else …

Why: _____
_____
_____

On the back of this page, you have a space for Journal notes including lines and even a place to draw about your experience. ↪

Additional Space To Write, Draw and/or Add Additional Thoughts or Memorabilia About Your Experience.

63

Date: _____

Description: _____
_____

Why I did this: _____
_____

Location (or where I completed): _____
_____

Who accompanied me: _____
_____

My thoughts: _____
_____
_____

My feelings: _____
_____
_____

Will I do it again:

☐ Yes … ☐ No … ☐ Maybe … ☐ Never … ☐ With someone … ☐ With someone else …

Why: _____
_____
_____

On the back of this page, you have a space for Journal notes including lines and even a place to draw about your experience. ⮐

Additional Space To Write, Draw and/or Add Additional Thoughts or Memorabilia About Your Experience.

64

Date: _____

Description: _____
_____

Why I did this: _____
_____

Location (or where I completed): _____
_____

Who accompanied me: _____
_____

My thoughts: _____
_____
_____

My feelings: _____
_____
_____

Will I do it again:

☐ Yes … ☐ No … ☐ Maybe … ☐ Never … ☐ With someone … ☐ With someone else …

Why: _____
_____
_____

On the back of this page, you have a space for Journal notes including lines and even a place to draw about your experience. ↪

Additional Space To Write, Draw and/or Add Additional Thoughts or Memorabilia About Your Experience.

65

Date: _____

Description: _____
_____

Why I did this: _____
_____

Location (or where I completed): _____
_____

Who accompanied me: _____
_____

My thoughts: _____
_____
_____

My feelings: _____
_____
_____

Will I do it again:

☐ Yes … ☐ No … ☐ Maybe … ☐ Never … ☐ With someone … ☐ With someone else …

Why: _____
_____
_____

On the back of this page, you have a space for Journal notes including lines and even a place to draw about your experience.

Additional Space To Write, Draw and/or Add Additional Thoughts or Memorabilia About Your Experience.

66

Date: _____

Description: _____
_____

Why I did this: _____
_____

Location (or where I completed): _____
_____

Who accompanied me: _____
_____

My thoughts: _____
_____
_____

My feelings: _____
_____
_____

Will I do it again:

☐ Yes … ☐ No … ☐ Maybe … ☐ Never … ☐ With someone … ☐ With someone else …

Why: _____
_____
_____

On the back of this page, you have a space for Journal notes including lines and even a place to draw about your experience. ⤴

Additional Space To Write, Draw and/or Add Additional Thoughts or Memorabilia About Your Experience.

67

Date: _____

Description: _____
_____

Why I did this: _____
_____

Location (or where I completed): _____
_____

Who accompanied me: _____
_____

My thoughts: _____
_____
_____

My feelings: _____
_____
_____

Will I do it again:

☐ Yes … ☐ No … ☐ Maybe … ☐ Never … ☐ With someone … ☐ With someone else …

Why: _____
_____
_____

On the back of this page, you have a space for Journal notes including lines and even a place to draw about your experience. ➲

Additional Space To Write, Draw and/or Add Additional Thoughts or Memorabilia About Your Experience.

68

Date: _____

Description: _____
_____

Why I did this: _____
_____

Location (or where I completed): _____
_____

Who accompanied me: _____
_____

My thoughts: _____
_____
_____

My feelings: _____
_____
_____

Will I do it again:

☐ Yes … ☐ No … ☐ Maybe … ☐ Never … ☐ With someone … ☐ With someone else …

Why: _____
_____
_____

On the back of this page, you have a space for Journal notes including lines and even a place to draw about your experience. ➲

Additional Space To Write, Draw and/or Add Additional Thoughts or Memorabilia About Your Experience.

69

Date: _____

Description: _____
_____

Why I did this: _____
_____

Location (or where I completed): _____
_____

Who accompanied me: _____
_____

My thoughts: _____
_____
_____

My feelings: _____
_____
_____

Will I do it again:

☐ Yes … ☐ No … ☐ Maybe … ☐ Never … ☐ With someone … ☐ With someone else …

Why: _____
_____
_____

On the back of this page, you have a space for Journal notes including lines and even a place to draw about your experience.

Additional Space To Write, Draw and/or Add Additional Thoughts or Memorabilia About Your Experience.

70

Date: _____

Description: _____
_____

Why I did this: _____
_____

Location (or where I completed): _____
_____

Who accompanied me: _____
_____

My thoughts: _____
_____
_____

My feelings: _____
_____
_____

Will I do it again:

☐ Yes … ☐ No … ☐ Maybe … ☐ Never … ☐ With someone … ☐ With someone else …

Why: _____
_____
_____

On the back of this page, you have a space for Journal notes including lines and even a place to draw about your experience. ↻

Additional Space To Write, Draw and/or Add Additional Thoughts or Memorabilia About Your Experience.

71

Date: _____

Description: _____
_____

Why I did this: _____
_____

Location (or where I completed): _____
_____

Who accompanied me: _____
_____

My thoughts: _____
_____
_____

My feelings: _____
_____
_____

Will I do it again:

☐ Yes … ☐ No … ☐ Maybe … ☐ Never … ☐ With someone … ☐ With someone else …

Why: _____
_____
_____

On the back of this page, you have a space for Journal notes including lines and even a place to draw about your experience.

Additional Space To Write, Draw and/or Add Additional Thoughts or Memorabilia About Your Experience.

72

Date: _____

Description: _____

_____

Why I did this: _____

_____

Location (or where I completed): _____

_____

Who accompanied me: _____

_____

My thoughts: _____

_____

_____

My feelings: _____

_____

_____

Will I do it again:

☐ Yes … ☐ No … ☐ Maybe … ☐ Never … ☐ With someone … ☐ With someone else …

Why: _____

_____

_____

On the back of this page, you have a space for Journal notes including lines and even a place to draw about your experience. ⮕

Additional Space To Write, Draw and/or Add Additional Thoughts or Memorabilia About Your Experience.

73

Date: _____

Description: _____
_____

Why I did this: _____
_____

Location (or where I completed): _____
_____

Who accompanied me: _____
_____

My thoughts: _____
_____
_____

My feelings: _____
_____
_____

Will I do it again:

☐ Yes … ☐ No … ☐ Maybe … ☐ Never … ☐ With someone … ☐ With someone else …

Why: _____
_____
_____

On the back of this page, you have a space for Journal notes including lines and even a place to draw about your experience.

Additional Space To Write, Draw and/or Add Additional Thoughts or Memorabilia About Your Experience.

#74

Date: _____

Description: _____
_____

Why I did this: _____
_____

Location (or where I completed): _____
_____

Who accompanied me: _____
_____

My thoughts: _____
_____
_____
_____

My feelings: _____
_____
_____
_____

Will I do it again:

☐ Yes … ☐ No … ☐ Maybe … ☐ Never … ☐ With someone … ☐ With someone else …

Why: _____
_____
_____

On the back of this page, you have a space for Journal notes including lines and even a place to draw about your experience.   ⮕

Additional Space To Write, Draw and/or Add Additional Thoughts or Memorabilia About Your Experience.

75

Date: _____

Description: _____
_____

Why I did this: _____
_____

Location (or where I completed): _____
_____

Who accompanied me: _____
_____

My thoughts: _____
_____
_____

My feelings: _____
_____
_____

Will I do it again:

☐ Yes … ☐ No … ☐ Maybe … ☐ Never … ☐ With someone … ☐ With someone else …

Why: _____
_____
_____

On the back of this page, you have a space for Journal notes including lines and even a place to draw about your experience. ➲

Additional Space To Write, Draw and/or Add Additional Thoughts or Memorabilia About Your Experience.

76

Date: _____

Description: _____
_____

Why I did this: _____
_____

Location (or where I completed): _____
_____

Who accompanied me: _____
_____

My thoughts: _____
_____
_____

My feelings: _____
_____
_____

Will I do it again:

☐ Yes … ☐ No … ☐ Maybe … ☐ Never … ☐ With someone … ☐ With someone else …

Why: _____
_____
_____

On the back of this page, you have a space for Journal notes including lines and even a place to draw about your experience. ↻

Additional Space To Write, Draw and/or Add Additional Thoughts or Memorabilia About Your Experience.

77

Date: _____

Description: _____
_____

Why I did this: _____
_____

Location (or where I completed): _____
_____

Who accompanied me: _____
_____

My thoughts: _____
_____
_____

My feelings: _____
_____
_____

Will I do it again:

☐ Yes … ☐ No … ☐ Maybe … ☐ Never … ☐ With someone … ☐ With someone else …

Why: _____
_____
_____

On the back of this page, you have a space for Journal notes including lines and even a place to draw about your experience. ➲

Additional Space To Write, Draw and/or Add Additional Thoughts or Memorabilia About Your Experience.

#78

Date: _____

Description: _____
_____

Why I did this: _____
_____

Location (or where I completed): _____
_____

Who accompanied me: _____
_____

My thoughts: _____
_____
_____

My feelings: _____
_____
_____

Will I do it again:

☐ Yes … ☐ No … ☐ Maybe … ☐ Never … ☐ With someone … ☐ With someone else …

Why: _____
_____
_____

On the back of this page, you have a space for Journal notes including lines and even a place to draw about your experience. ➲

Additional Space To Write, Draw and/or Add Additional Thoughts or Memorabilia About Your Experience.

#79

Date: _____

Description: _____
_____

Why I did this: _____
_____

Location (or where I completed): _____
_____

Who accompanied me: _____
_____

My thoughts: _____
_____
_____
_____

My feelings: _____
_____
_____
_____

Will I do it again:

☐ Yes … ☐ No … ☐ Maybe … ☐ Never … ☐ With someone … ☐ With someone else …

Why: _____
_____
_____

On the back of this page, you have a space for Journal notes including lines and even a place to draw about your experience. ➲

Additional Space To Write, Draw and/or Add Additional Thoughts or Memorabilia About Your Experience.

80

Date: _____

Description: _____
_____

Why I did this: _____
_____

Location (or where I completed): _____
_____

Who accompanied me: _____
_____

My thoughts: _____
_____
_____

My feelings: _____
_____
_____

Will I do it again:

☐ Yes … ☐ No … ☐ Maybe … ☐ Never … ☐ With someone … ☐ With someone else …

Why: _____
_____
_____

On the back of this page, you have a space for Journal notes including lines and even a place to draw about your experience. ➲

Additional Space To Write, Draw and/or Add Additional Thoughts or Memorabilia About Your Experience.

81

Date: _____

Description: _____
_____

Why I did this: _____
_____

Location (or where I completed): _____
_____

Who accompanied me: _____
_____

My thoughts: _____
_____
_____

My feelings: _____
_____
_____

Will I do it again:

☐ Yes … ☐ No … ☐ Maybe … ☐ Never … ☐ With someone … ☐ With someone else …

Why: _____
_____
_____

On the back of this page, you have a space for Journal notes including lines and even a place to draw about your experience.

Additional Space To Write, Draw and/or Add Additional Thoughts or Memorabilia About Your Experience.

82

Date: _____

Description: _____
_____

Why I did this: _____
_____

Location (or where I completed): _____
_____

Who accompanied me: _____
_____

My thoughts: _____
_____
_____

My feelings: _____
_____
_____

Will I do it again:

☐ Yes … ☐ No … ☐ Maybe … ☐ Never … ☐ With someone … ☐ With someone else …

Why: _____
_____
_____

On the back of this page, you have a space for Journal notes including lines and even a place to draw about your experience.

Additional Space To Write, Draw and/or Add Additional Thoughts or Memorabilia About Your Experience.

83

Date: _____

Description: _____
_____

Why I did this: _____
_____

Location (or where I completed): _____
_____

Who accompanied me: _____
_____

My thoughts: _____
_____
_____

My feelings: _____
_____
_____

Will I do it again:

☐ Yes … ☐ No … ☐ Maybe … ☐ Never … ☐ With someone … ☐ With someone else …

Why: _____
_____
_____

On the back of this page, you have a space for Journal notes including lines and even a place to draw about your experience. ➲

Additional Space To Write, Draw and/or Add Additional Thoughts or Memorabilia About Your Experience.

84

Date: _____

Description: _____
_____

Why I did this: _____
_____

Location (or where I completed): _____
_____

Who accompanied me: _____
_____

My thoughts: _____
_____
_____

My feelings: _____
_____
_____

Will I do it again:

☐ Yes … ☐ No … ☐ Maybe … ☐ Never … ☐ With someone … ☐ With someone else …

Why: _____
_____
_____

On the back of this page, you have a space for Journal notes including lines and even a place to draw about your experience. ➲

Additional Space To Write, Draw and/or Add Additional Thoughts or Memorabilia About Your Experience.

85

Date: _____

Description: _____
_____

Why I did this: _____
_____

Location (or where I completed): _____
_____

Who accompanied me: _____
_____

My thoughts: _____
_____
_____

My feelings: _____
_____
_____

Will I do it again:

☐ Yes … ☐ No … ☐ Maybe … ☐ Never … ☐ With someone … ☐ With someone else …

Why: _____
_____
_____

On the back of this page, you have a space for Journal notes including lines and even a place to draw about your experience.

Additional Space To Write, Draw and/or Add Additional Thoughts or Memorabilia About Your Experience.

#86

Date: _____

Description: _____
_____

Why I did this: _____
_____

Location (or where I completed): _____
_____

Who accompanied me: _____
_____

My thoughts: _____
_____
_____

My feelings: _____
_____
_____

Will I do it again:

☐ Yes … ☐ No … ☐ Maybe … ☐ Never … ☐ With someone … ☐ With someone else …

Why: _____
_____
_____

On the back of this page, you have a space for Journal notes including lines and even a place to draw about your experience. ➲

Additional Space To Write, Draw and/or Add Additional Thoughts or Memorabilia About Your Experience.

#87

Date: _____

Description: _____
_____

Why I did this: _____
_____

Location (or where I completed): _____
_____

Who accompanied me: _____
_____

My thoughts: _____
_____
_____

My feelings: _____
_____
_____

Will I do it again:

☐ Yes … ☐ No … ☐ Maybe … ☐ Never … ☐ With someone … ☐ With someone else …

Why: _____
_____
_____

On the back of this page, you have a space for Journal notes including lines and even a place to draw about your experience.

Additional Space To Write, Draw and/or Add Additional Thoughts or Memorabilia About Your Experience.

88

Date: _____

Description: _____
_____

Why I did this: _____
_____

Location (or where I completed): _____
_____

Who accompanied me: _____
_____

My thoughts: _____
_____
_____

My feelings: _____
_____
_____

Will I do it again:

☐ Yes … ☐ No … ☐ Maybe … ☐ Never … ☐ With someone … ☐ With someone else …

Why: _____
_____
_____

On the back of this page, you have a space for Journal notes including lines and even a place to draw about your experience.

Additional Space To Write, Draw and/or Add Additional Thoughts or Memorabilia About Your Experience.

89

Date: _____

Description: _____
_____

Why I did this: _____
_____

Location (or where I completed): _____
_____

Who accompanied me: _____
_____

My thoughts: _____
_____
_____
_____

My feelings: _____
_____
_____

Will I do it again:

☐ Yes … ☐ No … ☐ Maybe … ☐ Never … ☐ With someone … ☐ With someone else …

Why: _____
_____
_____

On the back of this page, you have a space for Journal notes including lines and even a place to draw about your experience.

Additional Space To Write, Draw and/or Add Additional Thoughts or Memorabilia About Your Experience.

90

Date: _____

Description: _____
_____

Why I did this: _____
_____

Location (or where I completed): _____
_____

Who accompanied me: _____
_____

My thoughts: _____
_____
_____

My feelings: _____
_____
_____

Will I do it again:

☐ Yes … ☐ No … ☐ Maybe … ☐ Never … ☐ With someone … ☐ With someone else …

Why: _____
_____
_____

On the back of this page, you have a space for Journal notes including lines and even a place to draw about your experience. ↩

Additional Space To Write, Draw and/or Add Additional Thoughts or Memorabilia About Your Experience.

91

Date: _____

Description: _____
_____

Why I did this: _____
_____

Location (or where I completed): _____
_____

Who accompanied me: _____
_____

My thoughts: _____
_____
_____

My feelings: _____
_____
_____

Will I do it again:

☐ Yes … ☐ No … ☐ Maybe … ☐ Never … ☐ With someone … ☐ With someone else …

Why: _____
_____
_____

On the back of this page, you have a space for Journal notes including lines and even a place to draw about your experience.

Additional Space To Write, Draw and/or Add Additional Thoughts or Memorabilia About Your Experience.

92

Date: _____

Description: _____
_____

Why I did this: _____
_____

Location (or where I completed): _____
_____

Who accompanied me: _____
_____

My thoughts: _____
_____
_____

My feelings: _____
_____
_____

Will I do it again:

☐ Yes … ☐ No … ☐ Maybe … ☐ Never … ☐ With someone … ☐ With someone else …

Why: _____
_____
_____

On the back of this page, you have a space for Journal notes including lines and even a place to draw about your experience. ↻

Additional Space To Write, Draw and/or Add Additional Thoughts or Memorabilia About Your Experience.

93

Date: _____

Description: _____
_____

Why I did this: _____
_____

Location (or where I completed): _____
_____

Who accompanied me: _____
_____

My thoughts: _____
_____
_____

My feelings: _____
_____
_____

Will I do it again:

☐ Yes … ☐ No … ☐ Maybe … ☐ Never … ☐ With someone … ☐ With someone else …

Why: _____
_____
_____

On the back of this page, you have a space for Journal notes including lines and even a place to draw about your experience.

Additional Space To Write, Draw and/or Add Additional Thoughts or Memorabilia About Your Experience.

94

Date: _____

Description: _____

_____

Why I did this: _____

_____

Location (or where I completed): _____

_____

Who accompanied me: _____

_____

My thoughts: _____

_____

_____

My feelings: _____

_____

_____

Will I do it again:

☐ Yes … ☐ No … ☐ Maybe … ☐ Never … ☐ With someone … ☐ With someone else …

Why: _____

_____

_____

On the back of this page, you have a space for Journal notes including lines and even a place to draw about your experience. ➲

Additional Space To Write, Draw and/or Add Additional Thoughts or Memorabilia About Your Experience.

#95

Date: _____

Description: _____
_____

Why I did this: _____
_____

Location (or where I completed): _____
_____

Who accompanied me: _____
_____

My thoughts: _____
_____
_____

My feelings: _____
_____
_____

Will I do it again:

☐ Yes … ☐ No … ☐ Maybe … ☐ Never … ☐ With someone … ☐ With someone else …

Why: _____
_____
_____

On the back of this page, you have a space for Journal notes including lines and even a place to draw about your experience. ⮌

Additional Space To Write, Draw and/or Add Additional Thoughts or Memorabilia About Your Experience.

96

Date: _____

Description: _____
_____

Why I did this: _____
_____

Location (or where I completed): _____
_____

Who accompanied me: _____
_____

My thoughts: _____
_____
_____

My feelings: _____
_____
_____

Will I do it again:

☐ Yes … ☐ No … ☐ Maybe … ☐ Never … ☐ With someone … ☐ With someone else …

Why: _____
_____
_____

On the back of this page, you have a space for Journal notes including lines and even a place to draw about your experience. ➲

Additional Space To Write, Draw and/or Add Additional Thoughts or Memorabilia About Your Experience.

97

Date: _____

Description: _____
_____

Why I did this: _____
_____

Location (or where I completed): _____
_____

Who accompanied me: _____
_____

My thoughts: _____
_____
_____

My feelings: _____
_____
_____

Will I do it again:

☐ Yes … ☐ No … ☐ Maybe … ☐ Never … ☐ With someone … ☐ With someone else …

Why: _____
_____
_____

On the back of this page, you have a space for Journal notes including lines and even a place to draw about your experience. ➲

Additional Space To Write, Draw and/or Add Additional Thoughts or Memorabilia About Your Experience.

#98

Date: _____

Description: _____
_____

Why I did this: _____
_____

Location (or where I completed): _____
_____

Who accompanied me: _____
_____

My thoughts: _____
_____
_____

My feelings: _____
_____
_____

Will I do it again:

☐ Yes … ☐ No … ☐ Maybe … ☐ Never … ☐ With someone … ☐ With someone else …

Why: _____
_____
_____

On the back of this page, you have a space for Journal notes including lines and even a place to draw about your experience. ⮂

Additional Space To Write, Draw and/or Add Additional Thoughts or Memorabilia About Your Experience.

99

Date: _____

Description: _____
_____

Why I did this: _____
_____

Location (or where I completed): _____
_____

Who accompanied me: _____
_____

My thoughts: _____
_____
_____

My feelings: _____
_____
_____

Will I do it again:

☐ Yes … ☐ No … ☐ Maybe … ☐ Never … ☐ With someone … ☐ With someone else …

Why: _____
_____
_____

On the back of this page, you have a space for Journal notes including lines and even a place to draw about your experience. ⮎

Additional Space To Write, Draw and/or Add Additional Thoughts or Memorabilia About Your Experience.

100

Date: _____

Description: _____
_____

Why I did this: _____
_____

Location (or where I completed): _____
_____

Who accompanied me: _____
_____

My thoughts: _____
_____
_____

My feelings: _____
_____
_____

Will I do it again:

☐ Yes … ☐ No … ☐ Maybe … ☐ Never … ☐ With someone … ☐ With someone else …

Why: _____
_____
_____

On the back of this page, you have a space for Journal notes including lines and even a place to draw about your experience. ➲

Additional Space To Write, Draw and/or Add Additional Thoughts or Memorabilia About Your Experience.

About the Author and Designer of this Book
Rosemary Augustine

A native of southern New Jersey, Rosemary Augustine spent most of her adult life living in California and Colorado and returned to the Philadelphia area in 2001 to care for an aging parent. Rosemary calls herself a Journal Aficionado (her License Plate reads: Journal) as she is an avid writer, including a daily journaling practice. She writes fiction and non-fiction books, and creates journals for daily use. Her artistic endeavors include acrylic painting and mixed media collages. She designs many of her books including both the covers and interior pages. Rosemary is the author of numerous books including *365 Days of Creative Writing* (365 Journal Prompts), *Journal to a More Creative Self*, *Secrets I Learned From Ordinary House Cats*, *Adventures with Byron*, *Ziggy's Secrets* (a password logbook) along with four books on career and business topics. Rosemary is listed in Who's Who of American Women and Who's Who in the World. You can read more about Rosemary and her artistic endeavors and published books at her website: www.RosemaryAugustine.com. In 2015. she relocated to Melbourne, FL with her famous cat "Ziggy" - who has his own Facebook page called: Ziggy's Secrets.

. . .

www.ingramcontent.com/pod-product-compliance
Lightning Source LLC
LaVergne TN
LVHW061345060426
835512LV00012B/2563